No Lex 12-12

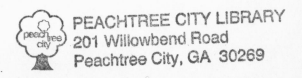

The Death of Gandhi

On January 30, 1948, Mohandas Karamchand Gandhi, spiritual leader of more than three hundred million Indians and spiritual idol of hundreds of millions of people throughout the world, met his death at the hands of an assassin. The world grieved that the frail Hindu (lovingly called *Mahatma,* or Great Soul, by his followers), who had preached passive resistance to force, courage in the face of oppression, and nonviolence as a response to evil, should meet so violent an end. Yet, in a very real sense, Gandhi's death embodied his triumph.

As the heart and soul of India's struggle for independence, Gandhi had always been much more than a mystic. His religious beliefs gave him the strength and showed him the way to be effective in this world. His road to Truth had been the path of active commitment to the social, economic, and political needs of the oppressed. First in South Africa against a powerful racist government, then in his beloved India against the mighty power of the British Empire, he had led seemingly hopeless revolutionary struggles for equality and freedom — and won.

But Gandhi's life and accomplishments can only be understood through the great and ancient culture from which he emerged. India, with her teeming millions, her age-old religions, her complex history as a battlefield of races and a womb of philosophies, her struggle for nationhood — this was the land that inspired Gandhi's vision and he was, in turn, inspired by it. Through Gandhi, India found her soul again and won her independence; and through his teachings, she gave the world a new means of effecting social and political change without resorting to violence. This means has come to be the weapon of oppressed people everywhere — it was Gandhi's legacy and his final triumph.

PRINCIPALS

GAUTAMA — Indian prince who founded Buddhist religion

ALEXANDER THE GREAT — King of Greece, conqueror of the Indian Northwest

ASOKA — Maurya Emperor of India (273–232 B.C.)

BABUR — Mogul conqueror of India

AKBAR — Mogul Emperor of India (A.D. 1556–1605) who ruled through righteousness

SHAH JAHAN — Mogul Emperor of India (1628–58) who built the Taj Mahal

AURANGZEB — Last great Mogul Emperor of India (1658–1707)

VASCO DA GAMA — Portuguese explorer

ROBERT CLIVE — English leader of the British East India Company forces

WARREN HASTINGS — English governor-general of Bengal

JAN CHRISTIAAN SMUTS — South African political leader

JAWAHARLAL NEHRU — Leader of the Indian National Congress

MOHAMMED ALI JINNAH — Leader of the Moslem League

LORD LOUIS MOUNTBATTEN — Last British viceroy of India

NATHURAM VINAYAK GODSE — Assassin

MOHANDAS KARAMCHAND GANDHI — Saintly Indian political leader

The Mahatma.

THE DEATH
OF GANDHI

JANUARY 30, 1948
India's Spiritual Leader Helps
His Nation Win Independence

By Robert Goldston

A World Focus Book

FRANKLIN WATTS, INC.
NEW YORK | 1973

COVER ILLUSTRATION BY GINGER GILES

PICTURE CREDITS

Charles Phelps Cushing: pp. 16, 29; Information Service of India: frontis, pp. 6, 13 (above), 21, 31, 37, 44, 49, 55, 58, 64, 69, 72, 80; Metropolitan Museum of Art, Purchase, 1969. Bequest of Florence Waterbury: p. 32; Sawders-Cushing: p. 26; U.P.I.: pp. 3, 9, 78 (above); Wide World Photos: pp. viii, 13 (below), 52, 76, 78 (below).

LIBRARY OF CONGRESS CATALOGING IN PUBLICATION DATA

Goldston, Robert C.
    The death of Gandhi.

    (A World Focus Book)
    SUMMARY: Traces the history of India and discusses Gandhi's life and his role in winning independence for his country.
    1. Gandhi, Mohandas Karamchand, 1869-1948–Juvenile literature. 2. India–History–Juvenile literature. [1. Gandhi, Mohandas Karamchand, 1869-1948. 2. India–History] I. Title.
DS481.G3G585   954.03′5′0924 [B] [92]   72-6074 ISBN 0-531-02160-2

Contents

Bombay, 1948. Soldiers of the Somerset Light Infantry, last British troops to leave India, on parade prior to their departure for England.

Prologue:
The Death
of an Empire

Perhaps it had always been inevitable that a great empire founded in blood must end in blood; perhaps there is some cosmic scale in history upon which the anguish of one generation must be balanced by the sorrow of the next. Certainly, by January, 1948, it had become painfully apparent that the end of British rule in India meant disaster; it had unleashed a terrible "holy war" such as had not been known since the Crusades. For more than one hundred and fifty years the British had been the "paramount power" in the vast and teeming Indian subcontinent; for nearly a century they had ruled it as "the brightest jewel of empire." Now the mighty *Raj* (British government in India) was crumbling, and its death had given birth to hatred, violence, and massacre.

The end of the Raj had been brought about by many factors. Of these, the most important were the rise of aggressive Indian nationalism and the exhaustion of British wealth and power through the fearful struggles of World War II. Britain simply could no longer afford the men, the material, and the money to maintain control. Furthermore, the waning of British power east of Suez had been accompanied by a growing realization in England that maintaining imperial pretensions in India was not only impractical but also ethically and morally wrong. As World War II drew to its conclusion, a majority of English people were very willing to support their government's efforts to withdraw. But, as Benjamin Franklin once observed about an-

1

other people long held in bondage, "Slavery is such an atrocious debasement of human nature that its very extirpation, if not performed with solicitous care, may sometimes open a source of serious evils." The extirpation of the bondage in which India had been held for generations was no exception.

Basically it was a question of what kind of India would now emerge. A land divided into more than five hundred petty states, more than a dozen major languages, and two major and many minor religions had been welded into one by British power. Now that power was being withdrawn and chaos threatened. The vast majority of Indians were Hindus, but a very substantial minority were Moslems. For many decades these two religious blocs had viewed each other with suspicion and growing hostility. Hindus dreamed of a united, free India ruled by democratic processes. But Moslems, realizing that a united India would be ruled by its Hindu majority, feared oppression and discrimination. They demanded the creation of a separate Moslem nation to be called Pakistan. Since historical accident had planted Moslem majorities in widely separated areas of the subcontinent, this meant the creation of both an East and a West Pakistan with nearly 1,000 miles of Hindu territory between. To Hindu leaders, such a solution seemed to threaten the future stability of the entire subcontinent. By August, 1947, tensions had risen to such a degree that neither Hindu, Moslem, nor British politicians were really able to control events.

Disaster had erupted on August 16, 1946 — labeled by Moslem League leader Mohammed Ali Jinnah as "Direct Action Day" to open the Moslem campaign for an independent Pakistan. On that day, armed gangs of Moslems swept through the Hindu districts of Calcutta and massacred more than five thousand men,

2

Police patrol rides through one of Calcutta's main streets following knife-fighting, looting, and arson in the wake of the Hindu-Moslem riots of 1946.

women, and children. Hindus in Calcutta and elsewhere in India replied by instituting terrible slaughters of Moslem men, women, and children. Soon rioting, accompanied by cruel atrocities, had spread through much of the nation. Organized Moslem gangs were countered by militant Hindu groups — and the faithful of both religions killed each other with the terrible fury of unleashed fanaticism.

By October, 1946, the killing had spread from Bengal to the province of Bihar. The crazed zealots of both sides cried "Blood for blood!" and many thousands died. Only the continued presence of British forces stemmed part of the horror — but it was obvious that these forces could no longer control an increasingly desperate situation.

In February, 1947, the British government finally announced that it would quit India not later than June, 1948. At that time the power of the Raj would be transferred to whatever organization the Indians had been able to set up in the meantime. But as massacres continued, breaking out now with renewed ferocity in the Punjab, it became apparent that Indian independence could not be postponed that long. Knowing that the Raj was withdrawing, fewer and fewer people were willing to obey its immediate orders. Thus, on August 15, 1947, British rule in India officially came to an end and, as had been foreseen, the British left behind them a nation divided. East and North Bengal formed the new nation of Pakistan, ruled by Jinnah's Moslem League. The rest of the subcontinent remained "India" and was ruled by the Hindus of the Congress Party led by Jawaharlal Nehru. But even independence and division did not bring peace to a tortured land.

With the splitting of the subcontinent into Pakistan and

4

India, many millions of people found themselves living on the wrong side of the borders — Moslems in Hindu India, Hindus in Moslem Pakistan. After all the bloodshed, few of these misplaced people were willing to trust their lives to governments composed of their enemies. They therefore took to the roads by the hundreds of thousands, carrying small bundles of possessions or pulling carts full of family belongings with them. More than eight million refugees crossed the borders in both directions in one of the greatest and most miserable mass migrations in human history.

But still the killing did not end. The miles-long refugee columns were attacked by rival gangs who were intent as much upon plunder as revenge; troops assigned to guard the refugee columns often attacked them too. Along the new borders between Pakistan and India fighting flared between the rival armies of the two nations. In October, 1947, an undeclared war broke out over which nation would rule the rich province of Kashmir — a land with a Moslem majority but a Hindu ruler. While both Pakistan's Jinnah and India's Nehru were, somewhat reluctantly, willing to allow the United Nations to mediate this dispute, neither of them could control the many millions of their followers who thirsted only for battle. The killings continued; massacres now broke out and Moslems perished by the thousands. The entire subcontinent stood on the threshold of anarchy and total civil war.

Neither the Indian nor the Pakistani police and armed forces could be trusted to maintain impartial order. The United Nations did not possess the means or the will to control the subcontinent's more than 350,000,000 people. Neither of the world's newly emerged super powers, the United States and the Soviet Union,

5

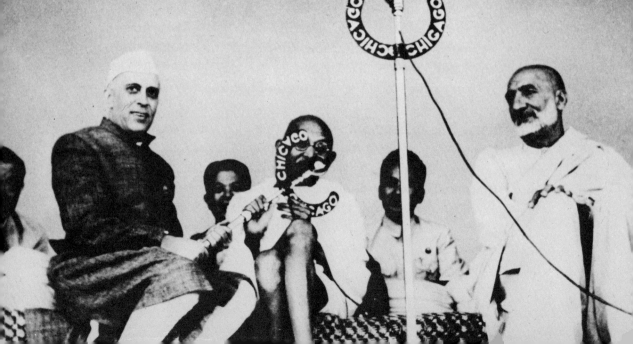

would permit the other to intervene to maintain peace — nor did either of them demonstrate any real interest in doing so. The only "force" in all the world that might be able to bring peace to a bleeding land was moral force — and it was expressed in one solitary, elderly, stooped individual.

This man, though born and raised a Hindu, was also a friend of Moslems, Jews, and Christians. He called all worshipers of God his brothers, no matter what their religion. He called those his brothers, too, who professed no religious belief at all. While Gandhi was an Indian who had devoted years of his life to combating the British Raj, he still bore the English no ill will whatsoever; indeed, he counted himself the brother of all people no matter what their nationality.

Although this man was revered by millions of people all over the world, he had no organized following at his command and no means of imposing his will on others even if he had desired to do so. His life was austere, his small wealth had been consumed by charities, and his physical health was frail. His only "weapons" were persuasion, love, and personal example. Many people thought of him as a saint who could do no wrong; others hated him as a charlatan. Some westerners loathed him as the man who, more than any other, had brought the white man's rule in India to an end. Most Moslems viewed him with suspicion as a

Above: Mahatma Gandhi with Lord and Lady Mountbatten at the Viceroy's house, New Delhi, in March, 1947. Details were then being worked out for Britain's leaving India. Below: Gandhi (center) is shown here with Jawaharlal Nehru (left) and Khan Abdul Ghaffar Khan (right) at the Asian Relations Conference in New Delhi, April, 1947.

Hindu; many Hindus distrusted him for not hating Moslems. The old were often fearful of following his way of passive resistance to evil; the young were often impatient with his precepts of non-violence.

Yet Mohandas Karamchand Gandhi, called *Mahatma* (Great Soul), did not see himself as a person worthy of either hatred or devotion. He offered his blessing to those who hated him and discouraged those who idolized him. He considered himself no more than a pilgrim upon the road to Truth — but a pilgrim who did not forget his responsibilities to his fellow men. When his beloved India was divided, when her teeming millions fell to slaughtering each other, his only means of influencing the dreadful chaos that threatened was a deeply personal one. On January 13, 1948, he embarked on a fast. No food or drink, he declared, would pass his lips until Hindus and Moslems recovered their sanity and made true peace. The killing must end, the hatred must be banished. If not, he would meet his God in anguish, unwilling to survive where so many had already perished.

Despite the tremendous moral authority encompassed in his frail body and the veneration in which he was held by so many, friends as well as enemies wondered if this example of his willingness to die in the cause of peace could possibly prove effective against the tidal wave of hatred that engulfed his nation. If so, many felt it would be no less than a miracle.

The Worldly Saint

The man from whom millions hoped for a miracle knew himself to be thoroughly mortal. Indeed, he had arrived at his religious conclusions largely through the experience of mundane, everyday

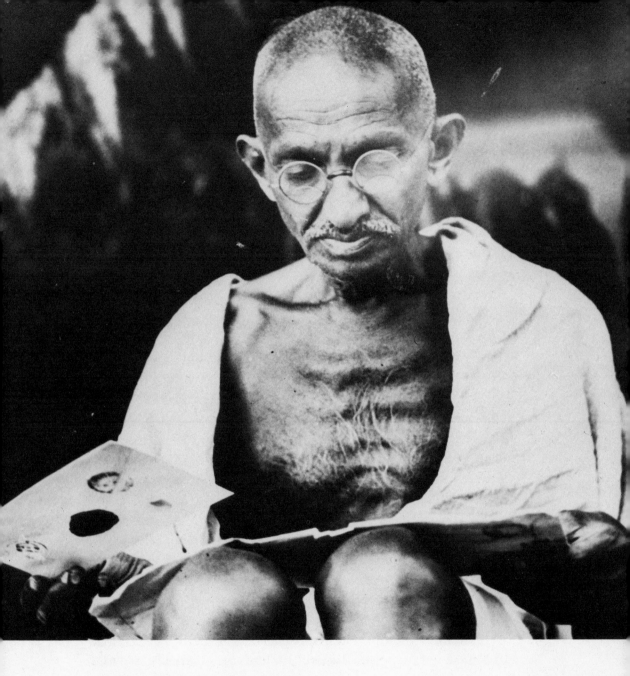

Gandhi prepares for a hunger strike.

affairs and especially from the jostling demands of practical political action. His uniqueness lay in the fact that he was able, in turn, to apply these religious conclusions to worldly problems.

Mohandas Gandhi was born in the city of Porbandar in the Indian west coast district of Gujarat on October 2, 1869. His father was prime minister to the *Rana* (Prince) of Porbandar, but this position was not so exalted as it might sound. For Porbandar was a tiny principality among hundreds whose affairs were really governed by British political agents. In 1869, just eleven years after the suppression of the Great Indian Mutiny, most of the subcontinent of India was a colony of the British Empire. The native Indian princes who were allowed to retain the pretense of sovereignty existed, as British Prime Minister George Canning had observed years before, "without political power but as royal instruments."

The Gandhi family was Hindu, belonging to the *Vaisya* caste of businessmen. They were prosperous by Indian standards, and Mohandas, like his two brothers, was able to attend the local private school (there were no public schools at that time in India) where all subjects, by decree of the British Raj, were taught in English. But Gandhi's mother, a devout Hindu, instilled in her son a deep respect for his native culture. The gap between the English school books and the Indian child was emphasized when, following ancient custom, Mohandas was married at the age of thirteen to the equally youthful daughter of a Porbandar merchant. Although Gandhi would later denounce the custom of child marriage, his own marriage was long and happy.

After a brief and unsuccessful term at the British-established college in nearby Bhainagar (not far from Bombay), Mohandas, with his family's blessing, decided to become a lawyer.

10

But to practice law effectively in British India he would have to study law in England — a prospect that delighted him but worried his mother and his superstitious caste-brethren. At last, having taken a vow not to indulge in meat or wine while abroad, Gandhi departed for England in September, 1888.

This first trip to England was very important in molding Gandhi's later thought. While he applied himself successfully to the study of law (he received his degree in June, 1891), he learned much more besides. His acquaintanceships widened from the small Indian community in London to include many English friends. These he first met through the English Vegetarian Society (a group to which a non-meat-eating Hindu would naturally be drawn). Actually vegetarianism in late nineteenth-century England was linked to many other reformist movements. It was largely through these friends and other newfound English friends that young Gandhi first learned of the struggle for increased political democracy, women's rights, more liberal education, and the rights of workers. Furthermore, since many of these same reformers had taken a deep interest in Indian affairs and Hindu culture, it was through them that Gandhi was first introduced to much of his own native heritage. For example, he first read many of the Hindu religious classics in English translations.

It was at this time, too, that Gandhi first came into contact with Christian theology in its more progressive forms. Many of his friends were Theosophists, whose motto was "There is no religion higher than Truth" and who sought to combine the moral and ethical precepts of all religions into one. It was through the influence of his Theosophist friends that Gandhi first studied (in English) the great Hindu religious work the *Bhagavad-Gita*. And it was also through them that he first read the Bible. He

11

found himself responding especially to Christ's Sermon on the Mount with its great precept of "Resist not evil."

From the Bible, Gandhi went on to study the Koran and found much to admire in Mohammedanism, particularly Mohammed's courage and simplicity — how the Prophet fasted, mended his own shoes, and patched his own cloak. From these studies Gandhi began to weave his own pattern of religious belief. In this, however, he at first made little progress. It proved to be not study and contemplation alone but action in the real world of men that would prove to be Gandhi's way to the Truth he sought.

When Mohandas Gandhi returned to India as a lawyer in 1891, he found very little employment for his newly won knowledge. In fact, after six months of law practice in Bombay he succeeded in getting only one case to handle. The alternative — to follow the family tradition of practicing politics in the corrupt court of the Rana of Porbandar — sickened him. So when, in 1893, he was approached by a firm of Indian Moslem merchants who needed a lawyer to help them untangle their business affairs in South Africa, he eagerly accepted the position. Once again, Gandhi bid good-bye to his wife and family and set out for a foreign land, unaware that South Africa was to be the crucible in which he and his beliefs would quickly mature.

In 1893, South Africa was still divided between British colonies and an independent Boer Republic established by the

Above: Mohandas Gandhi (right) is shown here two years before he departed for England to study law, with his brother Laxmidas. Below: Gandhi as a law student in England about the year 1889.

12

descendants of early Dutch settlers. Attracted by the coal, copper, gold, and diamond mines of the region, both British and Dutch, in their respective areas, had established a racist and terribly exploitative domination over the native African tribes, who were held in virtual slavery. When, in 1860, the native Zulus refused to work the sugar plantations, British and Boer companies had imported many thousands of Indians as indentured laborers. Indentured meant that these Indians were required by contract to work a fixed number of years in return for their passage, receiving only a scanty living in company barracks and a miserable salary; if they refused to fulfill their contracts they could be sent to prison.

Other Indians, seeking to escape bad times in their homeland, had emigrated to South Africa in search of business and trade opportunities. Unlike the "coolies" (the white term for indentured laborers), these independent Indians were often highly literate and cultured — through hard work and intelligence many of them became very successful, thereby arousing white fear and hatred against them. Some Indians in South Africa were rich, most were poor; some were Moslems, most were Hindus, but all were regarded as less than human by South Africa's white racist masters. After Gandhi himself had been ejected from railway coaches, thrown off stagecoaches, and kicked into the gutter a few times, he comprehended the situation, although he could never understand the unreasoning hatred behind it. In later years he remarked: "It has always been a mystery to me how men can feel themselves honored by the humiliation of their fellow beings."

As a literate, well-traveled lawyer, Gandhi soon found himself drawn with a few others into a movement to improve the lot of Indians in South Africa. He wrote letters to the newspapers defending the Indian viewpoint, spoke at public meetings protesting restrictive legislation, and started teaching English to his fellow Indians so that their protests might be more effective. His energy and generosity of spirit soon brought him the leadership of a growing movement to win human rights for Indians in racist South Africa. Soon he founded an Indian newspaper (teaching himself other Indian languages such as Tamil in order to communicate with those who spoke neither Hindi nor Gujarati) and established a farm to which destitute followers might repair. His sincerity won him the support of wealthy members of the Indian community and his example even gained followers (a handful but dedicated) among white South Africans.

The struggle was to be long, arduous, and complex; Gandhi had many a harsh lesson to learn. For example, Indians in South Africa were demanding their rights as British subjects; but this meant, to Gandhi, that they must also assume their responsibilities. So when Great Britain embarked on the War to crush the Boers in South Africa, Gandhi and his followers, while recognizing the base imperialistic motives behind the war, supported the British cause by forming a volunteer ambulance corps. While this earned them the thanks of British authorities, it still brought them no relief from oppression. In other words, Indians could not win their rights by cooperating with their oppressors.

On the other hand, they certainly could not win their rights through any kind of violent struggle. When Indians at the mines went on strike, the government would use any pretext whatsoever to employ armed force to crush them. Political skirmishing between Gandhi's followers and the increasingly restrictive South African government (at this time a British crown colony), in-

15

During the Zulu Rebellion of 1906, Gandhi (circled) served as a sergeant in a stretcher-bearer unit.

volving local strikes, protest meetings, lawsuits, and appeals to the British government in London, continued with little result for the next few years. The more vocal and politically conscious the Indians became, the more they were feared and hated by South Africa's whites. In short, the ways, means, and forms of striving for equality available and sometimes successful in a democratic society (such as England's) were not necessarily useful when the conflict could be defined in racist terms.

Matters reached a point of crisis in 1906 when the Transvaal government sought to enact a new Asian registration law, which would have the effect of making permanent the oppression of Indians and even excluding them from the country. Recognizing this new law as a final and absolute threat to the continued existence of the Indian community in South Africa, Gandhi and his followers determined to oppose it by every means at their command. But what would these means be? If cooperation and violent resistance alike were foredoomed to failure, how could they hope to win?

Gandhi and the Philosophy of *Satyagraha*

The urgency of this crisis crystallized certain ideas in Gandhi's mind. These ideas were partly religious, partly political. Hinduism itself contained the conception of nonresistance to evil. But this concept had been fortified for Gandhi by his reading of certain western thinkers. He had also encountered the view that governmental force might be opposed by nonviolent means in the works of the great Russian novelist and anarchist Leo

17

Tolstoi. From the writings of the American nonconformist Henry Thoreau, he gained renewed confidence in his belief that it was the individual's *moral duty* to refuse to comply with unjust laws. Many other sources for Gandhi's ideas might be cited; yet he developed them further than any of his predecessors and added to them from his personal faith and experience so that they became something new.

The great weapon Gandhi developed to combat South African oppression was a combination of passive resistance, nonviolence, and active defiance. Its Indian name was *Satyagraha,* meaning literally "Firmness in Truth." At the heart of Satyagraha lies a faith in the existence of absolute Truth — a human religious concept to which the practitioner must bear witness. If any particular situation is approached with faith in the Truth and with an open mind and in the spirit of love for one's fellow men — even one's oppressor's — then if that situation contains an absolute evil, it will be recognized. The evil must be absolute, not relative. Thus while South African restrictions on Indians simply oppressed them, they remained relatively evil, but when those same restrictions were expanded with the aim of denying Indians their existence, they became absolutely evil because they became anti-life, anti-God. Furthermore, the evil must be objectivized — it must be expressed as an objective fact and not simply as the wickedness of an oppressor's *intentions* or motives. Hence, while white South Africa's motive had always been the extermination of the Indian community, it was not until that motive had been objectivized in the real world as a fact of law that it could properly be opposed. Men's motives may, after all, change; in fact, the success of a campaign based on Satyagraha would bring this about.

18

Once evil is recognized as absolute and objective, then the duty of one believing in Satyagraha — known as a *Satyagrahi* — is to oppose it absolutely. He must be moved to say, as did Martin Luther centuries ago: "Here I stand, I cannot do otherwise." And, in fact, at his "moment of truth," a Satyagrahi cannot do otherwise emotionally, spiritually, or mentally. Yet to oppose evil one must not employ evil as a weapon. Violence of any kind is evil and merely leads to further debasement. Therefore a Satyagrahi employs passive resistance; that is, he simply refuses to obey the laws or commands that embody evil, nor will he cooperate with such restrictions in any way. He will not employ violence against evil. On the contrary, he will even passively suffer violence to be done to himself without striking back. This concept of nonviolence (in Sanskrit *Ahisma*) is not, however, to be thought of as cowardice. The Satyagrahi does not suffer evil to be done in silence. Indeed, he goes forth to meet it. He speaks out against it, demonstrates against it, and does all of the things that personally commit him to bear witness against evil. By so doing he probably invites the violence he is committed not to resist. In the end, however, because he is witnessing to Truth against absolute evil, and because Truth is indivisible, even the Satyagrahi's oppressors must come to understand the evil of which they make themselves the instruments and recoil from it. The victory of Satyagraha lies in the conversion, not the destruction or humiliation, of one's oppressors — for one's oppressors are people and all people sooner or later must respond to the Truth that is in them, however stifled.

Of course, the ways and means of Satyagraha did not burst suddenly into being all at once. They were developed painfully during an arduous struggle. Gandhi's first reaction to the law that

19

required all Indians to register and be fingerprinted was to lead his followers in simply refusing to do either. When police violence (including the arrest and imprisonment for several months of Gandhi and many of his followers) failed to force the Indians to comply, the Boer political leader Jan Christiaan Smuts promised that if they did comply the law would be revoked. Since part of Satyagraha was to assume that one's opponents are honorable men, Gandhi and his followers, after a year of resistance, went ahead and registered.

But it soon developed that the South African government had no intention of repealing the law; Smuts had lied. So Gandhi carried Satyagraha one step farther and led his compatriots in publicly burning their new registration cards. The government response to this was further police violence and imprisonment. But by this time the united action of South Africa's Indians, and the growing personal reputation of Gandhi, had attracted the attention of people and governments far beyond South Africa's shores. Public opinion in England, and in India too, brought pressure to bear upon those governments to take steps to bring South Africa's whites to their senses. And since South Africa was a part of the British Empire, this pressure was decisive. But it did not come from foreign sources only: more than a few whites both within and without the South African government had been forced to think. They had been forced to face the ugly moral truth that the hatred they expressed for others was only the hatred that consumed themselves. Satyagraha had demanded much of its followers — total self-control and the willingness to

Mohandas Gandhi is pictured here with his wife Kasturba on their return to India from South Africa.

die if need be — but in 1914 in South Africa the campaign had been won. The hateful Asiatic Registration Law quietly disappeared from the government's books and an Indian Relief Bill was enacted.

Later, under poorer leadership and harsher times, South Africa's Indians would lose almost all the gains they had won; South Africa was destined to become a racist state of the most malevolent type. Thus there were those who questioned whether Satyagraha had really won by converting its opponents. And there were those who pointed out that the campaign had been successful because of the government's restraint — after all, another government might have replied to Satyagraha by simply exterminating its followers. But on the eve of World War I these questions seemed unreal. Gandhi and his followers had won.

Of greater importance perhaps was the fact that Gandhi had, through his twenty years of struggle in South Africa, developed a method and a body of thought that might be applied to other problems; especially those that beset India under the British Raj. On July 18, 1914, Gandhi set sail for his native land once again (by way of England), and this time he was committed to her liberation. Yet, even though he was armed with Satyagraha, the task ahead appeared all but impossible.

Gandhi's "Mother India"— Geography, Climate, and Early Culture

Englishmen of the last century often asked: What is India?

They would answer their own question by remarking that

India was a "British creation." Behind the obvious chauvinism of their answer, there happened to be much truth. For there had never been a single unified nation called "India" that embraced all the vast subcontinent ruled by Britain. Nor has that huge landmass ever been the exclusive home of a single people or a single language or a single culture. India had always been, since its earliest times, a land of many different peoples, tongues, religions, and cultures.

Yet a glance at the map will show that India is, at least, a geographical unity. It is a wedge-shaped peninsula jutting out from Southern Asia into the Indian Ocean. It is separated from the rest of the continent by the towering peaks of the mighty Himalaya mountain range — aptly called the "roof of the world." For migration or conquest, the only practical routes into India are certain mountain passes in the northwest, the most famous of which is the Khyber Pass. While trade and commerce came to India primarily by sea (the ports of southern India were thriving a thousand years before the birth of Christ), until the coming of the Europeans in recent times no important migrations of peoples arrived by that route.

Mountains not only block India from the rest of Asia; the Vindhya range, which runs roughly east and west, also cuts the subcontinent itself in half. The north, watered by the great river systems of the Indus (from which the area received its name) in the west and the Ganges in the east, is a far different place from tropical southern India. While the northern climate varies between hot summers and relatively cool winters, the south is hot all year round. The winds called monsoons blow from the southwest across the subcontinent from June through September and in the opposite direction during January and February.

INDIA

WEST
PAKISTAN

JAMMU AND KASHMIR

• Srinagar

HIMACHAL
PRADESH

PUNJAB   • Simla
Chandigarh •

HARYANA

Delhi •   • Moradabad

Mathura •
Jaipur •   • Agra   UTTAR
                             PRADESH   NEPAL

RAJASTHAN   • Lucknow   SIKKIM
                                                                              BHUTAN   ASSAM
ARAVALLI HILLS   Benares   Jumna Ri.   NAGALAND
                                        (Varanasi)   Ganges Ri.   • Kohima
                          Allahabad • •   Shillong •
                          Mirzapur   • Patna   WEST   MANIPUR
I   N   D   I   A   • Murshidabad   BENGAL   EAST
                                                                                 PAKISTAN   TRIPURA
GUJARAT   BIHAR   WEST
Ahmedabad •   • Bhopal   BENGAL   BURMA
                   MADHYA PRADESH   Calcutta •
              VINDHYA

                                        Mahanadi Ri.

DIU •   Cuttack
DAMAN •   • Bhubaneswar
DADRA   ORISSA
NAGAR HAVELI
Bombay •   MAHARASHTRA

              DECCAN PLATEAU

                        • Hyderabad

GOA   ANDHRA PRADESH   INDIA

MYSORE

ARABIAN SEA   BAY OF   Andaman
                                                              BENGAL   Islands

Laccadive, Minicore   Bangalore •   • Madras
and Amindive Islands   Mysore •
                    Malabar Coast
                    KERALA   NILGIRI HILLS   • Pondicherry

                    TAMIL NADU

Trivandrum •   Nicobar
                                                                         Islands

                        CEYLON

INDIAN OCEAN

It would be hard to exaggerate the importance of the rain-bearing monsoons. They bring to the lands of the south (which has no mighty river system) the water upon which farming, and hence the lives of the people, depend. And even the north, despite the Indus and Ganges, which are fed by the snows of the Himalayas, depends upon the monsoons to water part of its very intensive agriculture. If the rains fail, the harvest will fail and people are likely to starve. For despite giant strides toward industrialization, India remains overwhelmingly an agricultural land. Furthermore, it is an agricultural land in which farming methods remain, by and large, pathetically primitive. Machinery such as pumps and tractors cost money; most Indian farmers have no money. Working very small plots of land (rarely larger than 2 acres), they consider themselves lucky to wring from their labor a bare subsistence for their families. Little is left over to sell for the cash necessary to invest in better farming methods. So, simply because Indian farmers have been poor, they remain poor.

The early inhabitants of India created a civilization long before recorded history. The fascinating ruins of their cities may still be seen near the Indus River. These people had a means of writing, but it has yet to be deciphered. Their culture was over-run and conquered about 1500 B.C. by a wave of nomadic peoples who penetrated the northwest mountain passes. These invaders, called Aryans after their common language-group, probably brought the Indus civilization to an end. But although they conquered the pre-Aryan inhabitants, the newcomers did not wipe

The subcontinent of India as it appeared politically after independence from Great Britain.

Territorial soldiers guard the Khyber Pass, most famous of the mountain passes to India in the northwest frontier.

them out; they ruled over them and eventually intermarried. While the Aryan language, Sanskrit, became dominant in northern India (and is used especially for religious literature and ceremonies to this day), pre-Aryan tongues also survived, especially in the south.

Hinduism, Caste System, and Buddhism

India's great religion, Hinduism (of which Buddhism is but a later offshoot), grew from the fusion of Aryan and pre-Aryan beliefs. Its earliest writings, the *Vedas* (hymns to the gods), were composed in Sanskrit about 1300 B.C. Since that time, Hinduism has undergone many changes. Like other religions, it has become overlayed with superstitions, cults, sects, and ceremonies; but its basic tenets remain essentially the same. Hinduism teaches that this life and this world, all that men call reality, is but an illusion. Indeed, even the worlds beyond this one, which men call "heavens," are part of the same illusion. And, as most of life testifies, this illusory reality is more or less filled with pain and suffering. Happiness consists of escaping these illusions. Beyond this world of pain less painful (because less illusory) heavens or existences await — but beyond even these lies the true reality in which all things are one.

According to Hinduist beliefs, it is the great object of all spiritual striving to return the individual soul to this reality, called *Nirvana,* where it achieves the complete peace of nonbeing. A person's soul may be reborn again and again within the realms of illusion, that is, the physical world. Depending upon his conduct during these earthly lives, his soul may migrate upon his physical death to a higher or lower place on the evolutionary scale. Thus the soul of a man of bad conduct might be reborn in the body of a dog, or even an insect, while the soul of a virtuous man might reappear in the body of a king or even, if he were especially selfless and righteous, in the being of a god. These ups and downs of reincarnation are not divine punishments or rewards; rather they are the natural outcome of behavior. A righteous man's soul breeds increased righteousness or selflessness so that it naturally migrates to a higher plane after his death, and vice versa. For example, there once lived a very virtuous and holy monk whose only failing was the inordinate pride he took in his beautiful cloak. When this holy monk died, his pride caused his soul to be reborn in the body of a louse inhabiting that same cloak. But the louse quickly perished, and since aside from this one vice the monk's soul had always been virtuous, he was then reborn in the being of a god. Actually, the highest attainment of all in Hinduism is not to have one's soul reborn at all but to escape the endless cycle of rebirth and illusion by having it become one with true reality, the state known as Nirvana.

Like other religions, Hinduism is almost inseparable from its web of social customs. The most notable of these in India is

Mute testimony to India's great religion is this ruined Hindu temple in southern India. Since its early beginnings, Hinduism has undergone many changes.

the system of caste. From the early days of the Aryan conquest (possibly the Aryans introduced the system as a means of governing the subdued pre-Aryan peoples), Indian society was divided into four general classes: *Brahmans* (the highest class, from which priests and intellectuals emerged); *Kshatriyas* (warriors and aristocrats); *Vaisyas* (farmers and businessmen); and *Sudras* (servants and laborers). Within these four major classes over the centuries, there developed hundreds of subclasses, or *castes*. Outside these castes remained a large group (perhaps those whom the Aryans could not originally subdue) known as *outcastes*. For these people the lowest occupations were reserved and they were regarded by all caste Indians as "untouchable." This caste system was supposedly rigid. A person was born into a caste and was supposed to confine himself to the occupations reserved to it. He could not marry outside his caste, he was expected to die in it, and his children's children would remain forever in it. Hindu religious beliefs reinforced this system. For example, it was held that the soul born into the body of an untouchable must necessarily have migrated from the body of a very wicked man, and for this reason its present bodily habitation should remain just that — untouchable.

In actual practice, many of the social rules and taboos of the caste system were often disregarded. People did marry outside their caste occasionally and sometimes did change their occupations. But the overall strict hierarchy of castes was self-perpetuating since it kept some people rich and others poor. Combined with Hindu religious beliefs regarding the "illusions" of reality, it made for a docile and passive population that was easily ruled.

Sacred cows are allowed to roam at will in India. An "untouchable" squats at right with baby, as other castes mingle in this busy street.

Buddhism emerged from Hinduism during the sixth century before Christ as the teachings of a *Brahman* (in this case a prince) named Gautama. Rejecting his opulent birthright, Gautama dedicated himself to seeking the truth as a humble pilgrim. He taught that escape from the endless suffering of reincarnation might be attained by any soul, regardless of caste. The means to this end was to be found neither in the extreme of worldly activism nor in the life of pure contemplation, but in a "middle path" combining both. Through righteous actions in this world and the contemplation of Truth, Gautama himself achieved Buddhahood (the word Buddhism means "enlightenment"). In the centuries after his death his followers developed an intricate religious and ceremonial structure with a monastic system, which flourished for many centuries in India. But the power of the Buddhist monks drew the envy and, eventually, the wrath of Indian rulers upon the religion. After the ninth century A.D. its power declined at home but remained great in Ceylon, China, Southeast Asia, and Japan, to which countries it had long since been exported.

It was during the time of Buddhism's ascendance in India (in 326 B.C.) that the Greeks, led by Alexander the Great, fought their way through the Near East and burst upon India over the northwest mountain passes. By this time the power of the Aryan rulers had long since decayed. India was divided into hundreds of petty, squabbling principalities and the Greeks were able to win a sizable domain in the northwest. But the empire of Alexan-

A bronze sixth-century Indian sculpture of Buddha, religious teacher and founder of Buddhism.

der the Great did not long survive his death; in India it gave way to a resurgence of native power under the Maurya tribes, whose kings soon extended their rule to most of the subcontinent.

Asoka and the Maurya Kings

By far the greatest of the Maurya kings was the Emperor Asoka (273–232 B.C.), whose court was famed for its patronage of the arts and learning and whose rule was noted for justice and righteousness. Declaring "all men are my children," Asoka undertook to construct dams and roads, build welfare centers and hospitals, and support worthy religious institutions. Although he maintained a huge army, Asoka preferred to extend his power through the example of his righteousness, and in this he was highly successful.

Later Maurya kings grew weaker and their empire shrank. They were unable to successfully oppose the waves of intruders who swept into India (always over those northwest passes) from about 200 B.C. to A.D. 300. These invasions followed a pattern. A conquering tribe would descend from the northwest and subdue the local principalities, but their rule would inevitably be swallowed up by the vast masses, the great distances, and the rich culture and religion of the subcontinent. Thus the Greeks returned to be followed by Persians and then by Huns; but all eventually merged into Indian civilization. Native Indian rulers, the Guptas, managed to create an empire like that of the Mauryas during the fourth and fifth centuries A.D., but it too decayed and was swept away by the coming of the Moslems.

Later Invaders—
the Moslems
and the Moguls

The Moslem invasion of India was unlike previous conquests. The Moslems did not sweep down all at once; instead, for many decades, they confined themselves to raiding from Afghanistan. The story of the Moslem conquest is one that extends over centuries. But by the year A.D. 1100, Moslem sultans ruled much of the northwest and much of the south from their great capital at Delhi. And, unlike other invaders, the Moslems, primarily because of their strong religious beliefs, did not allow themselves to be absorbed by the Indian civilization.

The great Moslem religion, with its roots in Judaism and Christianity, taught the existence of but one God (Allah) and one Prophet (Mohammed). All who did not accept Islam were infidels, who were to be converted by the sword, enslaved, or if they resisted, killed. The precepts of Hinduism and Buddhism were not simply foreign to the Moslems; they were hateful. Thus the Moslems (they were of various nationalities, predominantly from Asia Minor) ruled their Indian Empire as a conquered province. Their cities were armed camps from which they exploited the wealth of the land and enslaved its people. They never permitted their own religion or culture to be much modified by the "infidel" civilization over which they ruled.

The Islamic kingdoms of the early Moslem conquerors were overthrown in India in A.D. 1526 when the great warrior Babur led his Mogul (Mongol) forces to defeat the King of Delhi. Although themselves Moslems, the Moguls did not originate in the Near East but in north-central Asia. Babur himself claimed to be a direct descendant of Genghis Khan, whose hordes had conquered half the known world; he made himself the first Mogul Emperor of India. Later Mogul rulers expanded the empire until it embraced all of northern and central India and most of the south. Of the Mogul sovereigns, three were notable.

The first of these was Akbar (reign A.D. 1556–1605), who attempted to bring Moslems and Hindus together (he himself married a Hindu) and who did away with many of the harsher Moslem laws that held Hindus in subjection. Akbar's administration was famed for many reforms, but especially for his attempt to rechannel tax moneys back to native villages in the form of public works and improved agricultural methods.

Another well-remembered Mogul ruler was Shah Jahan (1628–58), whose interest in architecture helped develop the unique Mogul style. It was he who ordered the construction of one of the world's loveliest monuments, the Taj Mahal at Agra, as a tomb for his wife.

The last of the great Mogul rulers was the Emperor Aurangzeb (1658–1707), whose martial and political skills brought the Mogul dominion to its greatest power. A warrior of great intelligence and courage, Aurangzeb was still leading his armies personally at the age of eighty — and they remained victorious during his lifetime. He was harsher, more suspicious, and more anti-Hindu than his predecessors, largely because internal decay and rival claims to power now threatened the entire fabric of

The great Mogul ruler Akbar did away with many of the harsh Moslem laws that held Hindus in subjection. Old print depicts his custom of holding long talks with men of many faiths.

Mogul rule in India. Aurangzeb was able to hold the empire together and even to expand it, but when he died its disintegration was rapid.

The very extent of the Mogul Empire in an age before the development of rapid communication and transportation made it difficult to rule. Governors of remote provinces, appointed by the emperor at Delhi, had a way of growing independent and setting themselves up as supreme rulers within their local territories. And, too, certain of the Hindu kingdoms had never been completely subjugated. After the death of Aurangzeb, Hindu power in India revived. In the northwest, the Hindu Rajputs (who for decades had only been nominally under Mogul rule) established their complete independence. In the far south, the Mogul power, always weak, soon vanished. But of greatest importance was the rise of the Maratha Confederacy of Hindu principalities, which though mainly centered in the west stretched like a belt across the subcontinent. As Mogul power declined, the strength of the Maratha Confederacy expanded. By the middle of the eighteenth century, the confederacy was the most important political domain in India.

But by that time the once-great Mogul Empire had shrunk to an almost shadow existence. Having lost great stretches of territory to Persian invaders in 1739 and to a now-united Afghanistan in succeeding decades, the Mogul emperor who continued to live in splendor at Delhi exercised no more real power in India than any number of other petty Hindu kings. In fact, the huge land of India had once again reverted to a kaleidoscope of principalities, sultanates, kingdoms, and confederacies, all battling and intriguing against each other, unable to unite in any common task. While the essential culture of the people and their age-old religions remained, the political greatness of the past was, in the early eighteenth century, but a dim memory.

It was unfortunate that this period of decline in Indian power should have coincided with the sudden expansion of western power embodied in the new nation-states of Europe. Had India been able to present a united political and military front to the world, she might well have escaped her new conquerors — conquerors who, unlike all the many others she had known, were to come to her not over the northwest passes but over the sea.

The Course of Empire—European Conquerors in India

The first Europeans to arrive were the Portuguese. Seeking new trade routes to the fabled wealth of the Orient that would bypass the power of the near-eastern Moslem empires, Prince Henry the Navigator's captains pushed ever farther down the Atlantic coast of Africa. Then, in 1488, Bartholomeu Diaz rounded the Cape of Good Hope. Ten years later Vasco da Gama reached the Malabar (southwest) coast of India. When he landed, certain Indians asked him "What do you seek?" "Christians and spices" was his reply.

This answer illuminates the two principal motives for European penetration of the East during the following centuries. Although much wealth was to be made from trade, plunder, and commerce, a sincere and zealous desire to spread the Christian faith also motivated many of the early expeditions. Catholic

missionaries (Jesuits for the most part) were among the first European visitors to India. They were well received by Emperor Akbar himself.

For many decades India was not a primary lure for European traders — it was simply a convenient way station on the route to the Spice Islands (Moluccas), which today form part of the nation of Indonesia. From Indian ports, European fleets could also act to suppress the swarming Arab pirates of the Red Sea and the Indian Ocean. These ports also served as bases from which merchant fleets could be convoyed against the depredations of other European powers seeking to exploit the same trade routes. A little later it was found that Indian cloth, much prized by the inhabitants of the East Indies, made a valuable trading cargo to exchange for the peppers, spices, and rare woods sought by Europeans.

The Portuguese, first in the field, established stations on the Arabian peninsula, the Indian coasts, and the Malaysian peninsula. But Portugal was not powerful enough to protect its eastern empire against other European rivals. When Portugal was conquered by Spain in 1580, Philip II inherited the "bankrupt grocery business" that Portugal's empire had become. It was with the wealth wrung from this Oriental trade (as well as the silver of the New World) that Philip fought the Protestant Reformation in Europe and launched his "invincible" armada against Elizabethan England.

The defeat of Spain by England and Holland led to British and Dutch sea power supplanting that of Spain along the Oriental

The explorer Vasco da Gama, first European to discover the sea route to India.

trade routes. The Portuguese-Spanish stations in India, with one or two exceptions, were seized by English or Dutch expeditions. But still the great objective was not India itself; it was the wealth of the East Indies. Although England and Holland were sometimes allies in Europe, they competed in the East. It was because Holland succeeded in establishing permanent control over the East Indies that thwarted British ambitions turned to India as a source of wealth. By the end of the seventeenth century, France had joined England and Holland in the competition for Oriental trade. All three nations maintained military and trade strongholds on the Indian coasts.

At first, the European stations in India were merely trade and supply depots purchased or leased from local Indian rulers. Later, forts were built — not so much to defend the stations against local rulers as to defend them against roving bandit gangs, which the local Indian authorities were unable to suppress. The Mogul emperor had become, as has been seen, an all-but-powerless figurehead unable to ensure security throughout his decaying realms or even to enforce his will upon his local governors and tributary princes. Since the Europeans found themselves obliged to maintain their own security in the areas around their trading stations, it seemed fair that they be granted the right to tax local inhabitants, such grants being issued sometimes by the Mogul emperor but more often by his representatives, the local *nawabs*.

By the beginning of the eighteenth century, with Dutch energies diverted to the exploitation of the East Indies, England and France emerged as the two principal European rivals in India. Both nations were represented there by powerful government-chartered trading companies. These trading companies, composed of private merchants, had no desire to rule Indian territory — that would be an expensive undertaking. Rather, they were intent solely upon making as large a profit as possible. If they engaged in political intrigue or military activities, it was with the greatest reluctance and only as a means of securing their sources of wealth. The companies protected their stations and interests with native troops, called *sepoys,* recruited directly or rented from local Indian princes and officered by European mercenaries.

War in Europe between England and France also provoked war between the rival companies in India. The fighting flared fitfully from 1746 to 1760. Both countries were represented in India by remarkable men: the French by Joseph François Dupleix, governor of Pondicherry, and the British by Robert Clive, who started his career as a clerk with the British East India Company and rose to become governor of all its Indian possessions. The struggle between these rival companies was long and complex. It was a shifting kaleidoscope of intrigue and alliances with local Indian nawabs and princes, punctuated now and then with battles. The French were handicapped by a lack of money, by their home government's involvement in other areas, and, above all, by a lack of ships. They lost ground slowly but surely. At the battle of Plassey, in 1757, Robert Clive (by now an officer in the king's army as well as commander of the British East India Company's private forces) led 3,000 mercenaries and sepoys to defeat a combined French and sepoy force of 50,000 men — a defeat from which French prestige and power in India never recovered.

ROBERT·LORD·CLIVE·BARON·OF·PLASS
A·D·1764

The Growth of British Influence in India

The years following Plassey saw a remarkable growth of British influence throughout the subcontinent. Political intrigue, bribery, and corruption were the chief weapons used by British East India Company officials who played one Indian nawab against another, sometimes supporting, sometimes opposing the Mogul emperor at Delhi. By the end of the eighteenth century The Company (as it was simply known in India) had become the strongest single power in the area. It was stronger than any of the semi-independent nawabs, stronger than any of the independent princes (such as the Nizam of Hyderabad), stronger than the Maratha Confederacy, and stronger than the Mogul emperor. The only power before which The Company had to bow was that of the British government itself. At first, because The Company's revenues had become an important factor in the English home economy and later because it was recognized that national as well as commercial interests were at stake, the British government after 1800 took greater and greater control of Company affairs.

The first instrument of this increased control was a remarkable man named Warren Hastings. Like Clive, Hastings started his career as a Company clerk. His administrative ability soon

A statue of Robert Clive, known as "Clive of India," who rose from an obscure clerk in the British East India Company to become governor of all its Indian possessions.

won him the governorship of The Company's holdings in Bengal and a huge personal fortune. When, in 1773, the British Parliament passed a Regulating Act to better control Company policy, Hastings was appointed governor-general of all British holdings in India. At the same time the government appointed a Council to help him. The conduct of affairs in India was left to the East India Company; Hastings and his Council acted as supervisors and guardians of the crown's interests, still in Company employ although appointed by Parliament. Hastings introduced reforms in The Company's tax collection system and in its administration of Indian villages and lands. His primary purpose was to check the many abuses by which Company officers built illegal or semi-legal personal fortunes. Yet so corrupt was the entire administration of Company affairs (a corruption matched by the venality of Indian officials dealing with it) that Hastings himself was eventually brought to trial in England before the House of Lords on charges of extortion and bribery. He was acquitted, but his trial brought home to many Englishmen the pressing need for basic reforms in British practices in India.

One of the charges brought against The Company was that its local courts were unjust and corrupt — indeed, that in any case involving Indian claims against The Company, no Indian could hope to win. To remedy this, Parliament created a Supreme Court in Calcutta independent of The Company court system and appointed a chief justice who would head not only the Calcutta Supreme Court but be in overall charge of The Company courts. In another move to strengthen government control of The Company, Parliament in 1784 enacted a new India Act, which established a government-appointed Board of Control sitting in

London to supervise the activities and decisions of governors-general and their Councils in India.

If it seems strange that a private trading company should have established not only its own private army and navy but also a private tax-collection system and system of courts in a foreign land, it must be remembered that this was the only effective system of government available throughout much of India. Local rulers were often corrupt, cruel, and inefficient. The Company had undertaken to govern on their behalf originally simply to maintain sufficient order to carry on trade. But soon the local Indian nawabs and princes became no more than figureheads. Besides, through political intrigue and battle, The Company came into ever-larger tracts of territory, which it owned outright. It has been said that the British Empire was built in a state of absentmindedness; certainly British rule in India was established in an unforeseen and haphazard manner. Nevertheless, many Indians welcomed Company rule as an improvement over local despotism and chaos.

During the first half of the nineteenth century, through the usual means, The Company further expanded its holdings in India. Territory in the northwest and large areas in the south fell under Company control. In 1818 the power of the Maratha Confederacy was broken and their vast lands were placed under Company "protection." Politically, India remained a crazy-quilt patchwork. There were independent states, such as Hyderabad (the largest); there were states ruled by nawabs, peshwas, and princes, which were only nominally independent while under complete Company control; there were territories owned and ruled directly by The Company; and there were, increasingly, lands owned or controlled by the British crown, which were administered by The Company. And there remained, of course, the shadowy authority of the Mogul emperor, whose real sovereignty now extended only to the area around Delhi. But even in the independent states, as well as in the court of the Mogul emperor, it was British political agents and Company representatives who determined policy.

That all of this did not prove too great an expense to The Company was due to the fact that its Indian "government" extended only to the maintenance of law and order and the collection of taxes. The humanitarian notion that Company government might be responsible for such matters as public education or health or the improvement of agricultural methods never entered the heads of its directors. The East India Company's prime concern remained the making of a profit — and the Board of Control in London supervised Company policy with this in mind. While they might occasionally intervene to prevent the worst excesses of greed and exploitation, British government officials put The Company's welfare first. After all, The Company was not only a chief source of wealth to its own private investors (men of means with great political influences in London), it had also become a lucrative source of tax revenues to the British government itself.

Despite this situation, during the early years of the nine-

Above: Warren Hastings, governor-general of British territories in India from 1774 to 1784. Below: An early nineteenth-century Indian prince who, although nominally independent, was like many other rulers under the control of the British East India Company.

48

teenth century a new school of political thought was appearing in England. Led by James Mill (who wrote *History of India* published in 1818), this school, dubbed the "Utilitarians," held that government existed to provide the greatest amount of practical good for the greatest number of its subjects. Thus the effectiveness of British rule in India was to be measured not only by Company profits or government revenues, but also by such practical improvements as roads, hospitals, schools, and so forth that it provided for the masses. From Mill's time on, there would be an increasing body of opinion in England concerned with the well-being of the Indian people, a body of opinion that would gain in political strength until it eventually imposed its views upon the British government. Even as early as the mid-nineteenth century, catering to this body of opinion, British government spokesmen were claiming that their "true" mission in India was not so much the exploitation of the land as it was to bring "enlightenment" and "civilization" to the "benighted heathen" for their own good.

Yet, the once-great power of the British East India Company, established by intrigue and bloodshed, itself came to an end in a welter of bloodshed in 1857–1858. By that time The Company effectively ruled all of India with the unimportant exception of a few states, mainly in the south. This rule was maintained by thousands of Company officials and agents backed by a large army of sepoys, who were trained and led by British officers. But resentment against Company rule was widespread and growing.

There were many sources of discontent. The nawabs and princes were jealous of their vanished power; devoutly religious Indians felt that Christianity and English practices threatened their ancient beliefs (for example, the English were attempting to stamp out the practice of *sati*, a Hindu rite in which widows were burned alive on the funeral pyres of their dead husbands); many Indians in The Company's employ were resentful of the fact that simply because they were Indians they were kept in the lowest positions; and, finally, the great masses of peasants remained illiterate, impoverished, and tax ridden.

The Sepoy Rebellion

The spark that ignited this smoldering resentment came from the sepoy regiments. In 1856, a new rifle (the Enfield) was issued to sepoy troops. To load this weapon, the soldiers had to bite off the end of the cartridge before placing a bullet in the breech. Now it so happened that these cartridges were greased with cow or pig fat, and it was a heinous offense in both the Hindu and Moslem religions to put to one's mouth anything that came from the sacred cow or the impure pig. Thus, when the new cartridges were issued, regiment after regiment of sepoy troops mutinied. They would kill their British officers and then either take to the hills or raise the banner of full-scale revolt. The revolt was fueled by all the grievances mentioned above, and mutinous troops were often joined by masses of discontented peasants who rallied to nawabs eager to exploit the situation. The nominal leadership of the uprising was forced upon the formerly despised Mogul emperor. At Delhi, as elsewhere, British civilians — men, women, and children — were massacred with appalling ferocity.

The British, hastily forming all-English regiments from escaped officers and civilian volunteers, and aided by many sepoy regiments that had not mutinied, as well as reinforcements of regular British regiments rushed out from England, were able to suppress the revolt within a few months. This was due to many

of the same factors that had enabled the British to establish their rule in the first place. The rebels lacked discipline and organization; they could not form a united front and were amenable to bribes and threats; they were unprepared to rouse (except locally) India's slumbering millions; and they had nothing to offer that would be an improvement on British rule. Fighting was fierce but restricted to certain small areas. Rebel atrocities against the English were fully matched by indiscriminate massacres of Indians perpetrated by vengeful English forces, especially in the city of Lucknow. By the spring of 1858 the Great Indian Mutiny (also known as the Sepoy Rebellion) was suppressed — but so too was the East India Company.

For the Great Mutiny had demonstrated conclusively that India could no longer be administered by a private trading company. Accordingly, in 1858, the British government assumed direct responsibility; the East India Company passed out of existence, the Mogul emperor was deposed, as were rebellious nawabs and princes, and although certain local rulers retained nominal sovereignty (as they had under The Company), most of the subcontinent was declared a part of the British Empire. A secretary of state for India was established in London as a part of the British Cabinet and the governors-general, as Britain's supreme representatives, were now granted the title of viceroy.

A large bureaucracy soon grew up both in London and Delhi to administer the British Raj. Indians were not included in either the Secretary of State for Indian Affairs' staff in London or in the Viceroy's Council of State in India. Nor were they, at

Lithograph shows British troops storming the fortress of Delhi during the Sepoy Rebellion in 1857.

first, included in the local Councils appointed to govern Indian provinces. But an Indian Civil Service came into being and, by degrees, Indians were accepted for it. Competitive examinations were established, and although top Civil Service posts were reserved for Englishmen, Indians soon won lesser positions. The Indian Army was reorganized and officered by regular British Army officers, and a British Army in India, composed entirely of English troops, was established.

When, eventually, Queen Victoria was proclaimed Empress of India in the last decades of the nineteenth century, it seemed that the huge subcontinent and its many diverse peoples had passed finally and irrevocably into the hands of its new conquerors. This was the India into which Mohandas Gandhi was born in 1869 — and this was the India to which he returned from South Africa in 1914.

The Struggle for India After 1914

From the return of Gandhi to his native land in 1914 to the birth of a free India more than thirty years later, a great struggle went on. It was not only a struggle for power between Britain and Indian rebels; it was also a struggle on Gandhi's part (and that of his followers) to educate, emancipate, and energize an entire people. In a very real sense it was a struggle for the soul of India.

Gandhi is shown outside his law office in South Africa in 1913, shortly before his return to India.

54

To understand this struggle it is necessary to understand the states of mind of the two opponents.

When the British penetrated India they found a land in complete political decay; indeed, it was that very decay that enabled them to gain complete power. But beyond that the British also found a land in social, religious, and moral decay. The caste system, with its ferocious extremes of wealth and poverty, its prejudices and vicious discriminations, was a symptom of social ossification on a far deeper level than the mere corruption of Indian officials. Over the centuries Hinduism itself had turned into a jumble of superstitious rituals and had become enmeshed in meaningless and often debased rites and beliefs — for example, the hideous practice of sati and the custom of child marriage. An example of both social and religious decay was the way in which the Hindu worship of the earth-mother goddess Kali by her devotees, called Thugs, had degenerated into a society of murderers and bandits. The vast masses of the population were illiterate, undernourished, ravaged by widespread disease, and sunk in lethargy.

The few sparks of economic and social vitality remaining in India had been stamped out by British policy. For example, the very large home and village manufacture of cloth, upon which India's local economy rested, was wiped out by a flood of imported British textiles, which were cheaper and better than those produced in India itself. As early as 1834, Lord William Bentinck, the governor-general, remarked that the bones of the cotton weavers were "bleaching in the plains." And since British policy was to preserve India as a source of raw materials and as a huge captive market for British manufactured goods, local industry was discouraged; in fact, what there was of it was generally British-financed, British-managed, and British-owned.

Looking upon their Indian Empire and its many millions of people, the British (with the exception of a very, very few) could honestly congratulate themselves that they were bringing the "benefits of civilization" to "a half-savage" land. Although these benefits — the hospitals, the schools and colleges, the postal system, the telegraphs and railroads, law and order, and so on — hardly touched the vast masses of India, not even that small token would have existed without the British Raj. Indians, as the state of their society demonstrated, were "inferior" people — at worst "debased and degenerate Asiatics" to be sternly governed, at best "naïve children" to be enlightened. When these "inferior" people rebelled against British domination (which was "for their own good"), the English rulers of India were confused, shocked, and outraged.

For Gandhi and his associates, the problem was much more complex than it was for the British. Their aim was not simply to win independence; it was to create a nation where none had ever existed before. This meant that the masses of India must be educated and inspired by a vision that would be as universal as possible and yet fully comprehensible. The people of India had to win back their self-respect first before they could throw off the British Raj. From India's past and her ancient culture and religion, elements would have to be drawn that would unite, educate, vitalize; only then could she liberate her people from their passivity and fatalism. If that could be accomplished, then a nation would come into being, and the British Raj would become irrelevant.

There were grounds upon which both the British and the Indians could meet. As the new century wore on, increasing numbers of thoughtful Englishmen came to recognize the true value of Indian art, philosophy, and religion. They also came to respect the people being ruled in their name. At the same time, many Englishmen were coming to realize that the same forces holding India in bondage were those that maintained economic and social oppression at home in England. Englishmen struggling for greater democracy at home and a more equitable distribution of their nation's wealth, found themselves natural allies of Indian "rebels."

Simultaneously many Indians had grown to appreciate the real worth of certain British values, traditions, and contributions. Most of India's leaders, including Gandhi, Nehru, and Jinnah, had received English educations. They admired English democracy (in its theory more than its practice), the hard-won rights embodied in the English Common Law, English ideas about fair play and decency. Indeed, at first they asked only that these very real benefits be applied in India as they were at home. They appealed beyond the British Raj to the British people and British traditions. And it was only when they became convinced that Britain would never apply English ideals to her Indian subjects that they demanded complete independence.

Indian nationalism, as a consciously organized political movement, had several sources, but it was most importantly embodied in the Indian National Congress founded in 1885. This Congress was first brought into being under British auspices. By

A portrait of Swindranath Banergee, one of the founders of the Indian National Congress, in 1885.

59

providing a "tame" outlet for the growing resentment of the handful of educated, "westernized" Indians, the British hoped to see the Congress become a harmless "safety valve." And for some years the Congress worked just that way; its membership was limited to the very few Indian intellectuals and its programs were mild suggestions for reform. Specifically, before 1900, the Congress asked for greater Indian participation in the British Raj. But as it increased its membership and as English officials showed themselves unwilling to undertake any real reforms, the Congress line began to harden. After the turn of the century Congress politicians were demanding complete Home Rule for India and dominion status (such as Canada and Australia enjoyed) within the British Empire.

The British unwittingly fostered the rise of Indian nationalism in two ways. First of all, the introduction of a common educational system (even though it was English and limited to the rich) and the introduction of telegraphs and the building of railroads were uniting India, providing a field in which nationalism might flourish. And secondly, British reluctance and tardiness in introducing reforms increasingly angered Indian leaders and caused them to distrust English promises and motives.

But if the British, who had not forgotten the Great Mutiny, feared that too rapid or too widespread reforms might open the floodgates to the nightmare of a general uprising by the impoverished masses, Congress leaders worried about how to reach those very masses — how to bridge the gap between sophisticated political action and India's illiterate, dispirited millions. Yet one Indian leader had done just that. Mohandas Gandhi, in distant South Africa, had managed to unite the large Indian community there. This was especially important because Congress itself was now disunited. India's Moslem leaders, distrusting the Hindu majority in Congress, had founded a separate Moslem League in 1906. And the Hindus themselves were splitting between fiery activists who looked forward to armed revolution and those (the majority) who preferred peaceful development. So high was Gandhi's reputation among India's political leaders by the time of his return in 1914 that they offered him the presidency of Congress immediately. But the *Mahatma* (as he was now being called, not for his political triumphs but for his religious ideals) declined the offer. After such a prolonged absence from his native land, he felt the need to spend some time in reacquainting himself with its present problems, movements, and dreams.

Gandhi's travels through India during the next few years convinced him that the British Raj must go. Unlike many Indian politicians, he visited both the urban slums and the depressed country villages. What he saw of poverty, despair, disease, and famine appalled him. Yet these were the conditions under which the vast majority of Indians survived. It was this depressed mass that had to be lifted, vitalized, and made an integral part of the movement for independence. The nuances of political maneuvering were far beyond the comprehension of the illiterate masses, but their ancient religious traditions, however debased, were not. Gandhi's unique position as a near-saint won him the respect and love of India's people to an extent that no mere politician could hope for. In turn, he realized that political action in India would have to be based upon and infused with religious ideals. In that way, the masses could regenerate themselves from their own cultural sources as they strove for freedom.

The means Gandhi would use to do this was Satyagraha, a social and political weapon derived from the deepest and purest

Hindu traditions, which all Indians could understand. But the practice of Satyagraha demanded complete self-discipline in non-violence. Were Indians ready for that?

Gandhi determined to give Satyagraha a try in 1918 in the district of Kheda. There, despite famine conditions, the government was attempting to collect its usual heavy taxes. Gandhi went to Kheda and persuaded most of the peasants to refuse to pay their taxes. The government responded by seizing the crops and pitiful belongings of the villagers. But the villagers, under Gandhi's firm leadership, offered no resistance and even cheered and sang as they were hustled off to jail. After a few months, the government gave up and remitted the taxes.

The year 1918 was the last year of World War I, a war into which India had been dragged by Britain. Hundreds of thousands of Indian soldiers served on the Western Front in Europe and many died there. Forced loans and increased taxes to support the war effort had reduced many Indians to destitution. A world-wide influenza epidemic as the war ended brought death to more than thirteen million Indians. But when Indian leaders, inspired by American President Woodrow Wilson's talk of "self-determination" for all nations, appealed for relief, the British Raj responded by passing new and harsher laws to control them.

Gandhi decided that this was another case for Satyagraha, which this time would take the form of a one-day nationwide general strike. As was his custom, he warned the British authorities of what he planned to do. On April 6, 1919, in the cities and in hundreds of thousands of villages, untold millions of Indians simply refused to work. But in some areas, provoked by police brutality, Indians rioted. Shops were looted, English people were assaulted and killed, private homes were burned. In the town of

Amritsar in the Punjab, after the initial violence had subsided and the city was calm, British authorities instituted a police massacre, which took the lives of nearly four hundred Indians and wounded more than one thousand. If India and the world were appalled by this, Gandhi was even more distressed. It was evident that many (perhaps most) Indians were not yet ready to practice satyagraha. "In the name of Satyagraha," he declared, "we have burnt down buildings, forcibly captured weapons, extorted money, stopped trains, cut off telegraph wires, killed innocent people and plundered shops and private houses." He immediately undertook a three-day fast to atone for this and called off his Satyagraha campaign. Greater thought, deeper indoctrination in the principles of nonviolence would be necessary before this peaceful weapon could be employed.

During the next few months, Gandhi worked out a new strategy to confront the British. This was his policy of noncooperation. Through it, Indians would simply withdraw from any and all activities that helped the Raj or made use of its institutions. Thus students would withdraw from schools and colleges, lawyers would cease to practice before the British courts, businessmen would stop dealing with English firms and individuals, peasants would stop selling their crops to the English, Indians would refuse to buy any English products, and eventually (though not immediately) Indians would refuse to pay taxes.

At the same time Indians would create their own schools, law courts, and commercial ventures. They would manufacture as many items as possible at home, especially cloth. In this way, while striking a blow at the Raj, they would be winning self-sufficiency and disciplining themselves for the future. And this program had the advantage that it broke no British laws outright

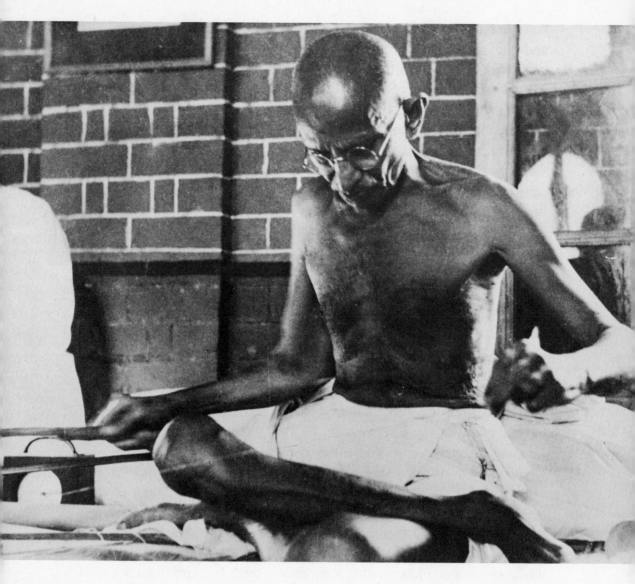

Gandhi's spinning wheel came to symbolize his movement. He is shown here at the wheel in later years.

and could be gradually stepped up by stages as the people grew more and more conscious of their power. Nor did it provide any excuse or outlet for violence. The Congress leaders heartily endorsed Gandhi's proposals and in January, 1921, the campaign of noncooperation began.

The program was highly successful. As always, Gandhi personally led the way, purchasing a spinning wheel and spinning his own yarn for half an hour each day. Soon the old-fashioned spinning wheel came to symbolize Gandhi's movement — and Indian pride and self-sufficiency, too. The government found it hard to cope with this campaign of noncooperation. No laws were being overtly broken, but the Raj was grinding to a halt as its activities were simply ignored by the Indian people. And, of even greater importance, English pockets were really feeling the Indian boycott of English manufactured goods.

But once again it was shown that India was not yet fully prepared for nonviolence. After several months of noncooperation, the industrial workers in several cities went out on strike. In Bombay, violence erupted and fifty-eight were killed in November. The British began arresting Congress leaders and further violence developed. On February 5, 1922, a mob in Gorakhpur retaliated against police brutality by massacring twenty-two policemen. This time, unlike the disturbances in Amritsar in 1919, all India was prepared for revolution. The campaign of noncooperation had created unity and organization among the masses.

Gandhi had only to give the word and the Raj would be faced by an immense and probably unsuppressible uprising. But Gandhi refused to give that word. In the face of reports of violence he went on a fast until the violence ceased; then he called off the more militant features of the noncooperation campaign. For the only time in recorded human history, a revolutionary leader who stood on the verge of success called off his revolution because he was morally and ethically convinced it would be the wrong kind of revolution. Rather than lead India into bloodshed, Gandhi preferred to fail.

The Mahatma was jailed by the British in March, 1922, after a trial at which his eloquence (he pleaded guilty, as always) moved even the English judge to sympathy. He was sentenced to six years' imprisonment, but his eloquent courtroom speeches, spreading across India, restored the prestige he had lost among the more militant of his followers when he called off the noncooperation campaign. The British learned from this error; later they imprisoned him again, but without a trial.

When Gandhi was released from prison in February, 1924 (his term was shortened because of ill health and British reluctance to create a martyr), he found that one of his most treasured dreams — a real and continuing alliance between India's Moslems and Hindus — had finally shattered. It was largely in hopes of repairing this that he accepted, in December, 1924, his one and only term (of one year) as president of the National Congress. But this was not the only split that troubled him. Increasingly, it had become clear to him that the Congress political leaders, despite their best intentions, had failed to make real contact with the great masses. Therefore, as president of Congress, he made them take up spinning and spend more time visiting villages and slums. And if the breach between Moslems and Hindus was beyond repair, at least, under the Mahatma's guidance, Congress leadership grew much closer to the Indian people. Gandhi's ideas of Satyagraha, brought to the people by hundreds of his disciples and preached endlessly through his newspaper articles and books, were beginning to be more fully comprehended.

In 1930, Gandhi judged that the time had arrived to strike another blow for freedom. By this time, Indian frustration and disappointment with unkept British political promises had led them to change their demand from Home Rule to outright independence. Once again civil disobedience, within the framework of Satyagraha, was to be the means. Gandhi seized at first upon one law that he considered totally unjust, the law that gave the British Raj a complete monopoly of the production of salt and forbade unlicensed Indians from producing, distributing, or using salt not produced under government license and taxes. On March 2, 1930, Gandhi wrote to the viceroy, as was his custom, explaining how and why he and his followers were going to break the salt laws.

On March 12, Gandhi and seventy-eight disciples started to march from his communal farm to the sea, 241 miles away. They were joined by thousands and, on April 6, Gandhi was the first to scoop up sea salt. Soon sea salt was being gathered, refined, and distributed throughout India in direct violation of the law. The Raj, bewildered at first, soon reacted violently. Police killed hundreds of Indians throughout the land in sporadic outbursts of violence; arrests included many of the top leaders of Congress and, on May 4, Gandhi himself was taken. But this time Indians did not fight back against the British. During all the violence directed against them, Indians did not kill one single Englishman. At last the lesson of Satyagraha had apparently been learned.

The civil disobedience of the salt marchers was now taken

up in other ways. The boycott of English cloth and other manufactures was intensified. When the Raj resorted to police force, Indians responded by holding general strikes, which hurt the British economy. Within a year, the British government in India was in confused retreat, while the British government at home had agreed to hold a Round Table Conference in London to sort out India's problems. Gandhi and the other Indian leaders were released from jail and, in the autumn of 1931, Gandhi traveled to England to attend the conference.

It was on this trip to London that Gandhi renewed his many friendships with English, American, and European supporters and admirers. Surrounded wherever he went by newsmen and cameramen as well as throngs of well-wishers, the Mahatma made skillful use of his opportunity to appeal to the English people and to such British intellectuals as George Bernard Shaw (an old acquaintance) over the head of the British government. But despite his personal success in establishing personal contact with many westerners of all degrees (he stayed in a London settlement house for the poor and spent an uncomfortable half hour taking tea with King George V), the conference he had come to attend was a total failure. Beset by the worldwide depression of the 1930's, Britain was unprepared to give up the "brightest jewel of Empire." Gandhi returned to India late in 1931 having accomplished nothing concrete.

Within a few days of the Mahatma's return, the British Raj struck. He and almost all of his immediate followers were jailed; all Congress Party leaders were imprisoned. The Congress Party was declared illegal and the police now turned to breaking strikes and boycotts with a vengeance. More than 32,000 people were arrested during January and February alone. So severe was the

Above: Mohandas Gandhi on his famous "salt march" in 1930. Below: Gandhi at the Round Table Conference in London.

repression that it seemed that the back of the Indian nationalist movement had at last been broken. Every weapon in the armory of state power, from censorship to public floggings, was employed. Deprived of top leadership, the Indian people were confused. Demoralization set in. And at this juncture the British brought forward a new plan for an Indian Constitution. Under its provision, India would not enjoy independence in any sense — only increased Home Rule. Combining this lure with their heavy-handed repression, the British authorities thought to finally stamp out Satyagraha.

But the newly proposed constitution contained a measure that Gandhi judged to be absolutely evil. This was a provision whereby India's Untouchables were to have segregated voting and representation in the new Legislative Assembly. Gandhi had devoted much of his life to attempting to break down the caste prejudices against Untouchables. The British now proposed to institutionalize them. When appeals to the Raj to reconsider the measure were fruitless, the imprisoned Mahatma went on a fast in his prison cell. He announced that he would thereby kill himself unless the British withdrew the measure — *and unless all Indians of whatever caste or religion displayed solidarity and brotherly love for the despised Untouchables.*

On September 20, 1932, Gandhi began his fast. He was sixty-three years old and his health failed rapidly. But now a near miracle occurred. So great was the esteem and love in which Gandhi was held by his fellow countrymen that high-caste Hindu temples were thrown open to Untouchables all over India; rich Brahmans ate with Untouchables in the streets; wealthy businessmen contributed all they owned to Untouchables; huge public gatherings declared their solidarity with Untouchables — and, by September 26, the British Raj, the British Home Government, and Indian political leaders all agreed that the measure that discriminated against Untouchables would be amended. Gandhi accepted orange juice. The caste system and Untouchability were not ended, but they would never be the same again. Above all, this victory restored the vanished morale of India's people.

When he was again released from prison in August, 1933, Gandhi decided to devote his energies to a direct and personal attack on Untouchability. The campaign of civil disobedience had petered out with the grudging acceptance of political reforms granted under the new constitution, reforms that gave the National Congress Party and other native political groups a chance to participate actively in government on the provincial level and even, to a limited extent, on the national. In 1935 the new Indian Constitution was approved by the British Parliament, and in 1937 elections were held that were easily won by Congress Party candidates, except for those seats reserved for Moslems and filled by candidates of the Moslem League. If India was moving toward self-rule (there was no suggestion at all that the British would accept independence), it was also moving toward a fatal division between its Hindu majority and the Moslem minority. Although Gandhi was able to make headway against Untouchability, he was unable to bridge that yawning abyss.

The coming of World War II brought Indian-British relations once again to the point of crisis. Fighting for her very life against Nazi Germany, and with the threat of Japanese aggression in the Far East a probability, the British demanded complete Indian support for their war effort. But although India

Gandhi with Sardar Vallabhai Patel and other Congress leaders in the early 1940s.

declared war on Germany and Italy, and the regular Indian Army regiments went off to fight all over the world, many Indian leaders pointed out that they could promise complete support only if they were truly free to give it. Many of the Congress Party leaders saw Britain's danger as their opportunity. After the Japanese attacked in 1941, Britain was unwilling to take any risks with her Indian Empire. In August, 1942, charging them with subversion and sabotage, the British arrested Congress Party leaders and once again drove the nationalist movement underground. Gandhi and Nehru were arrested with the rest, presumably because their continued agitation for independence threatened the Raj.

But there were some Indians at least who felt closer to the Japanese, an Asiatic people fighting against western imperialists, than to the British. Unable to see in Japanese militarism and aggression the same imperialist spirit that had subdued them, a handful of Indians joined the enemy. This provided the Raj with an excuse to clamp down on innocent and guilty alike.

Gandhi, sick with malaria, was released from prison in May, 1944. His childhood wife, Kasturbai, who had gone to prison with him had died there. As the Japanese tide retreated in Asia, British repression in India relaxed; by 1945, with complete victory in sight, the Raj had released almost all the imprisoned leaders and was once again negotiating with them on the thorny questions of Home Rule, independence, and the political structure of postwar India.

But by now there was a notable difference in British attitudes. Much had happened since Gandhi returned to India from South Africa in 1914. If Indians had matured politically and socially, Britain itself looked at a changed world through very different eyes. It now seemed that a majority of Englishmen were ready to dismantle the Raj and close the book of empire. If English attitudes were conditioned by the waning of British power in the dawning atomic age, they were conditioned too by lessons they had learned from a frail, ascetic, kindly saint. After many vicissitudes and disappointments, it seemed that in the end Satyagraha had achieved its ultimate purpose — the conversion of its opponents.

But if the now-apparent willingness of Britain to grant Indian independence brought satisfaction, it also caused alarm. The age-old distrust between Moslem and Hindu communities had never been resolved. Indian independence could very well lead to a fragmentation of the nation and to bloody civil war.

Epilogue:
The Tardy Miracle

When Gandhi embarked on his fast on January 13, 1948, the terrible violence sweeping across India and Pakistan seemed to mark the utter ruin of his teachings on Satyagraha. To court death through starving his body was not simply a means of exerting pressure upon those who loved, revered, or feared him. It had never been simply that. It was also both a means of purifying his own soul through mortifying his flesh and a way of focusing his attentions on the Truth that for him was God. If, as he hoped, he could serve as the instrument of Truth, he must be worthy of it. If his teachings failed, it could only be because in some way he had himself offended against Truth. By sharing, in his own manner, the suffering of many, he might redeem himself and show the way to the redemption of all.

74

The fast was addressed to the consciences of both Hindus and Moslems. It called upon them to pause and reflect. If they recovered their sanity, if amends were made to the victims insofar as this was possible, if brotherly love could triumph over blind hatred, then life might be worth living again.

The fast affected him quickly. He was now nearly seventy-nine years old. His weight (always slight) dropped rapidly; his kidneys no longer functioned — water made him nauseous. He spent most of his time on a cot on the front porch of his house, his knees drawn up, a white cloth covering everything except his patient face. Hundreds of visitors — Indians, westerners, and Pakistanis — filed past with prayers, tears, and entreaties to him to end his fast. It was very much as if the true worth and nature of Jesus of Nazareth had been recognized by all the world of his time, and representatives had begged him to escape the crucifixion he foresaw that evening in Gethsemane.

Gandhi, his voice a bare whisper, dictated a letter adding to his demands. There must be peace in Kashmir. The Indian government was holding on to 550,000,000 rupees, Pakistan's share of the assets of undivided India; this money must be handed over. Jawaharlal Nehru's government handed the money over immediately to Pakistan. The Pakistani foreign minister, addressing the Security Council of the United Nations, said that as a result of the fast, a "new and tremendous wave of feeling and desire for friendship" was sweeping the subcontinent. The leaders of some of the more militant Hindu groups (those who had taken the initiative in persecuting Moslems) assured Gandhi with tears in their eyes that they would not only stop all violence but would make amends and give assurances that such events would not be

repeated in the future. Pledges of the same sort came in from Moslem Pakistan.

On January 18, just five days after he had started his fast, Gandhi consented to end it. In just five days his example, relying on purity of motive and the love in which he was held by his people, had brought peace to a troubled land. His miracle had been accomplished, nonetheless real for having come after a prolonged agony.

And the miracle worked itself out with inexorable logic. For if peace had been imposed, yet not all hatred had been stilled in every heart. There were still Hindus and Moslems who desired nothing but each other's blood and only restrained themselves for fear of the Mahatma's moral authority. One of these was a thirty-five-year-old Hindu Brahman named Nathuram Vinayak Godse, editor of an inflammatory, radical newspaper in Poona. Godse considered Gandhi a traitor to Hinduism because of his concern for the Moslem minority in India; the success of Gandhi's fast had driven Godse to desperation.

On Friday, January 30, 1948, Gandhi spent the morning answering letters from friends, politicians, and religious leaders. His correspondence had been, for years, worldwide. In the afternoon he received an American journalist, who asked him what he would advise people to do if an airplane dropped an atomic bomb upon their city. Gandhi had already warned of the moral danger in even manufacturing such weapons. If such a thing

This picture, believed to be the last taken of Gandhi before his assassination a few days later, shows the Mahatma, weak from fasting, being assisted at a shrine in New Delhi.

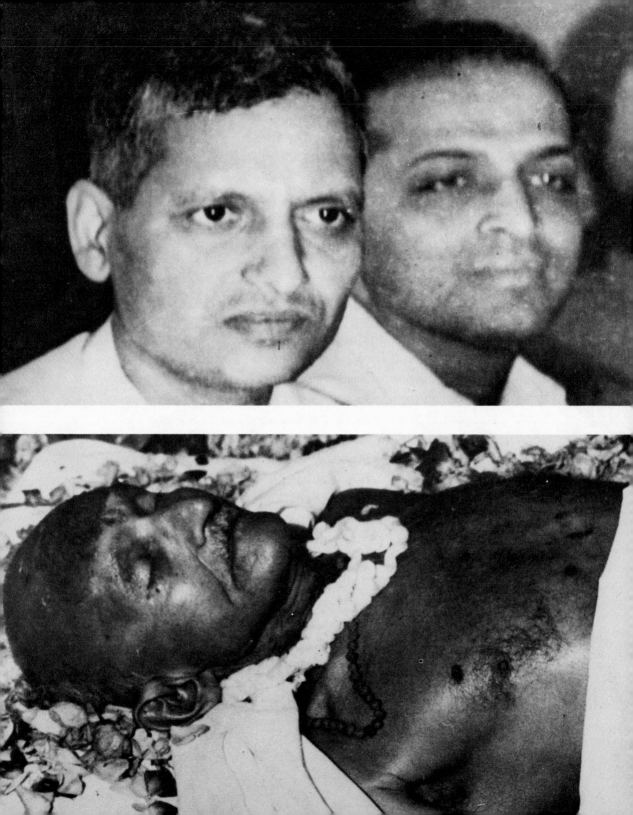

happened, he said, then the people should not seek shelter. They should stand firm, without fear, and pray for the soul of the pilot. Their sacrifice would not be in vain.

In the cool of the evening, around 5:00 P.M., Gandhi went out into his garden to lead his followers in their daily evening prayers. About five hundred people had gathered there. As the Mahatma appeared they stood up. Suddenly from their midst burst Nathuram Godse, revolver in hand. He fired three shots, and Gandhi sank beneath them, gasping the word "Rama," the divine Hindu name of God. He died within minutes.

Gandhi's death — a Hindu martyr for the rights of Moslems — put the final seal on the miracle his fast had begun. Overwhelmed with grief, India and Pakistan returned to the paths of peace; persecutions and threats ended; the war clouds dispersed.

Of course, peace, brotherly love, and communal understanding were not and have never been permanent conditions of mankind. The basis of all life is change, and, therefore, there can never be a permanently ideal society. But Gandhi taught men how to change their societies without violence. Not everyone could follow his path to its bitter end. Some have pointed out that Satyagraha was effective because Gandhi's opponents, the South Africans and the British, operated under self-imposed restraints.

What, for instance, would have been the result if Gandhi's

Above: The assassins of Mohandas Gandhi on trial. Actual assassin was Nathuram Godse, left. Narrayan Apte (right) was leader of the plot. Below: Covered with rose petals, the body of Mohandas Gandhi lies in state in the Birla House, New Delhi.

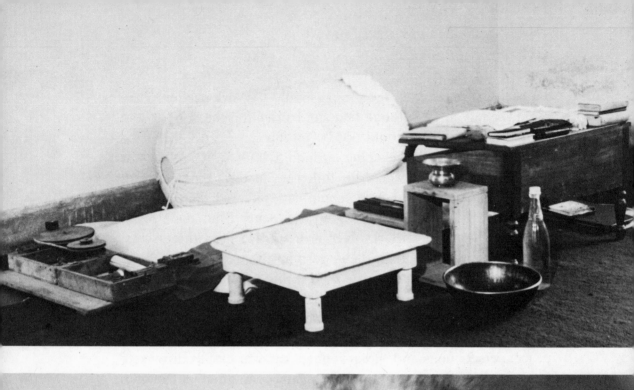

methods of passive resistance and civil disobedience had been practiced against Hitler's Germany; would not the Nazis simply have exterminated all three hundred million Indians if necessary? Perhaps, Gandhi might have replied, but their sacrifice, in the balance of divine Truth, would not have been in vain. Eventually, the murderers themselves would have tired, repented, and been converted. For Gandhi refused to believe in the triumph of evil — and this was his strength, his victory, his sainthood.

Above: Gathered here after his death are Gandhi's few possessions — his books, writing desk, spinning wheel, and other items. Below: Gandhi's funeral pyre ablaze. The Mahatma's ashes were subsequently carried to a final immersion ceremony in the holy Ganges River at the Sangam, Allahabad.

Chronology

B.C.

c. 2000 — Indus civilization flourishing in India

c. 1500 — Aryan tribes conquer most of India

c. 1300 — The *Vedas* (Hindu religious texts) written in Aryan Sanskrit

c. 550 — Prince Gautama teaches doctrines later known as Buddhism

326 — Alexander the Great leads Greek army into India

317 — Maurya dynasty of kings achieves supremacy in India

c. 280 — New wave of Greek invaders conquers northwest

c. 100 — Persians and Scythians conquer Indian northwest

A.D.

320 — Gupta kings establish their supremacy in India

465 — The Huns invade India

1206 — Moslems from Turkey establish supremacy over north India

1398 — Mongol hordes led by Tamerlane ravage India

1498 — Portuguese explorer Vasco da Gama reaches India

1526 — Babur defeats Sultan of Delhi and establishes Mogul Empire

1580 — Spain takes over Portuguese holdings in India

1660 — England and Holland compete for trade supremacy in India

1677 — France establishes trading posts in India

1757 — English and French battle for commercial supremacy in India

82

1773 — Warren Hastings becomes first governor-general of British East India Company territories in India

1784 — Warren Hastings is impeached before the House of Lords. Parliament establishes Board of Control over East India Company affairs

1857 — Great Indian Mutiny breaks out

1858 — Mutiny suppressed; East India Company holdings and power in India taken over directly by British government. India becomes a British possession as part of the empire

1869 — Mohandas K. Gandhi born

1885 — Indian National Congress formed under British auspices

1888 — Gandhi goes to England to study law

1891 — Gandhi returns to India

1893 — Gandhi goes to South Africa

1899 — Boer War between England and the Boer republics breaks out

1906 — Gandhi leads *Satyagraha* campaign against South African government for Indian rights. The Moslem League founded in India

1909 — Parliament, through the Government of India Act, grants increased Indian participation in Indian government

1914 — Gandhi's Satyagraha campaign in South Africa is successful

1914 — Gandhi returns to India

1918 — Parliament offers "dual rule" principle to India

1919 — Rioting at Amritsar bloodily suppressed by British Army

1920 — Indian leaders adopt Gandhian policy of noncooperation with British in India

1929 — Jawaharlal Nehru becomes president of 2nd National Congress, demands complete independence for India

1930 — Indian civil disobedience movement led by Gandhi and Congress

1937 — National Congress and Moslem League compete for seats in the central legislature

1941 — Britain at war with Japan

1942 — Japanese forces advance through Burma to Indian frontier. The Sir Stafford Cripps mission offers India greater independence after the war

1945 — A Labor Party government committed to end British rule in India is elected in England

1946 — Rioting between Hindus and Moslems breaks out in India

February,
1947 — British government announces that India will be independent not later than June, 1948. Lord Louis Mountbatten appointed viceroy to India. Terrible rioting continues

August 15,
1947 — British rule in India ends. Subcontinent divided into nations of India and Pakistan. Rioting and massacre continue

October,
1947 — India and Pakistan fight over possession of Kashmir

January 13,
1948 — Gandhi embarks on a fast to bring peace to India and Pakistan

January 18,
1948 — On the promise of peace, Gandhi ends his fast

January 30,
1948 — Mohandas Gandhi dies, victim of an assassin

Thereafter — Gandhi all but deified in his native India; his ideas on passive resistance and nonviolence in use by oppressed people throughout the world

Index

About the Author

A native New Yorker and a graduate of Columbia University, Robert Goldston is the author of over thirty books for children and four adult novels. Now living and writing in Ibiza, Balearic Islands, his literary interests include such subjects as Spain and its many upheavals, the Russian and French revolutions, and the history of the Far East. For Franklin Watts, Inc., Mr. Goldston has written *Pearl Harbor, The Long March, The Fall of the Winter Palace,* and *The Siege of the Alcazar.*